B♦TCH

Bad Words Made Funny Book 4

(I know... Why the fuck is there 4 of these horrible books?)

By Virginia Johnson

Graphic Design

Anytime Author Promotions

Kate Roberts – Cover Design

Proof Editing

Shelby West

The Legal Shit

In other words... Don't steal my shit!

Dedication

This book goes out to all the bitches that made it possible. Without you, we wouldn't have anyone to bitch about in our spare time.

Table of Contents

Graphic Design

The Legal Shit

Dedication

Table of Contents

Why Bitch?

Spanish

Arabic

French

Dutch

Mongolian

Russian

Persian

Bulgarian

Welsh

Norwegian

Hebrew

Swedish

Romanian

Chinese

Hungarian

Korean

Japanese

Finnish

Czech

Hindi

Polish

Somali

Maltese

German

Bosnian

English

Zulu

Greek

Thai

Estonian

Turkish

Italian

Bengali

Portuguese

Hmong

Kazakh

Uzbek

Icelandic

Cebuano

Latin

What have we learned?

Seriously?

About the Author

Why Bitch?

The chapter title itself is a question to the verb part of this word versus the noun. Let's address this one first. Bitch. Better yet, to bitch or not to bitch?

If you have a bad day, like stub your toe on the pitchfork that you left laying on the floor after your latest tirade against someone or something that didn't need you, that would make you bitch. It would also make you a bitch, but this is a reason to bitch. Not a good one, mind you. See, what you have to realize is that if you are going to bitch, you must have your shit together. If your bitch is a bunch of random words, thrown together to somehow justify your stance on something, step off your broken ladder and try again.

Here is an example of something to bitch about. You wake up in the morning and you realize that your car has been egged. This may seem like a rare occurrence, but it fucking happens. The little shit that lives down the block isn't very happy with you. (I am going to assume the asshole kid to be a boy, cause I can.) You, more than likely, tapped in to his attempt to bully on social media, called him a little bitch and made him cry himself to sleep. This kid googled ways to get back at you. So, instead of being an adult and sleeping with your significant other, this kid is forced to egg your fucking car.

You really should be grateful. He could have toilet papered your car, too. That shit is a bitch to get off, just saying.

Back to it. You have a legitimate reason to bitch in this situation.

Another way to bitch, and the most highly abused form of bitching, is being no different than the little shit that you called names to. You can be a keyboard warrior for the masses! Not really the masses, just the freedom fighter cause of the day. You know who you are and... so do we.

Bitching for attention is my favorite. "I am done! I am never doing this again." We have all heard this and some of us have reacted to this trap. Yeah, I called it a trap. *Poor me + your reaction = intended result.* The main problem here, is the result. The words that leave your mouth mean too many fucking things. You force your friends and family into a guessing game. Is it real? Is it fake? Did her (yeah, I am assuming the bitching is heard in a female voice) boyfriend/husband make her do it? Did she... see too much shit already!

What the bitching should have been is, "Give me attention, NOWWWWWWWW!" At least this way, the smart people around you get something out of it. I want to see an all-out tantrum as you beg for attention. You all know someone that has done it, if not, it is you.

Pat yourself on the back and kiss any self-respect you had for yourself goodbye. The raised eyebrows are not shock at your proclaimed demise. No... it is concern for your safety and those around you. Your bitching has caused the people around you to place tissues at your feet and begged you to not be so hard on yourself. Normal people around you are hoping that either you grow the fuck up or taste bleach – just enough for you to not want to do it again. Bitch, it will teach you a lesson.

Let's get this right, I am not encouraging self-harm, although it would give you something more to bitch about, but I am saying that you should stop bitching about bitching.

The only thing worse than bitching, is coming face to face with a(noun) bitch. Not just any bitch, but one that feels the need to be a bitch to be cool. Admit it, the one person, the popular kid, was a bitch. She probably spent her entire day drowning in her own sorrows, only to go home to every amenity made possible to humans. The only reason the bitch is a bitch is because mommy and daddy trained her to bitch.

A bitch learns from an early age. Having everything done for them is something they have grown to expect. I do blame the bitch. This is not the parents fault that this person exists. It isn't! No parent in their right mind wakes up one morning and says, "I think I want an entitled asshole living under this roof. We will ensure that she is socially awkward, rude to everyone she meets and let's count on her dropping out of school."

For the sake of the offended, I am going to address the Hollywood Bitch. The cheerleading captain, full of angst and condescending rage. You know her – again, if you don't, your friends think it's you. The shallow and whiny bitch that is covered in a painted façade that normal people call makeup. They only date within their social circle, mostly because everyone outside of them couldn't tolerate the bullshit for more than 20 minutes.

I will say, after twenty minutes, the visions of tearing vocal cords from a corpse start to surface, we have killed them three times and we are almost positive that we can hide the body in a trunk. Thankfully, many of us have parents that didn't want to raise serial killers so we tune out the bitch!

Anyways, whether you bitch, identify as a bitch or are an actual bitch – many people don't get away with referring to you as a bitch (The female dog thing was worn out in the 90's. No getting that back) which is why I decided to write this ridiculous book and give you new ways to say B*TCH. The languages are endless, confirming the 'bitch' status is global. Like an epidemic. Maybe one day they will research a cure; a serum capable of curing bitch-ism.

Fuck it, bitch... time to read on!

Spanish

Perra

(I thought it was puta – but apparently that belongs to the Galacian language)

SKILL PRACTICE

_____

_____

_____

_____

_____

_____

_____

_____

_____

Arabic

الكلبة

SKILL PRACTICE

_____

_____

_____

_____

_____

_____

_____

_____

_____

_____

_____

Virginia Johnson

French

Chienne

SKILL PRACTICE

_____

_____

_____

_____

_____

_____

_____

_____

_____

_____

_____

_____

_____

_____

Dutch

Teef

(I hear it is a very bad thing to be called in Dutch. Keep this in mind when you travel)

I want to call someone this for reaction purpose only.

My wonderful (Dutch) PA, Janneke, told me that if I value my hair and face, I should definitely NOT call a woman that! HAHAHAHAHA

SKILL PRACTICE

_____

_____

_____

_____

_____

_____

_____

_____

_____

_____

_____

_____

Virginia Johnson

Mongolian

Гичий

SKILL PRACTICE

_____

_____

_____

_____

_____

_____

_____

_____

_____

_____

Russian

Сука

SKILL PRACTICE

Virginia Johnson

Persian

عوضی

SKILL PRACTICE

Bulgarian

Кучка

SKILL PRACTICE

Virginia Johnson

Welsh

Bys

SKILL PRACTICE

_____

_____

_____

_____

_____

_____

_____

_____

Norwegian

Tispe

(I swear, I thought they were drinking!)

SKILL PRACTICE
_____

_____

_____

_____

_____

_____

_____

_____

_____

Virginia Johnson

Hebrew

כַּלְבָּה

SKILL PRACTICE

_____

_____

_____

_____

_____

_____

_____

_____

_____

Swedish

Tik

SKILL PRACTICE

Virginia Johnson

Romanian

Căţea

SKILL PRACTICE

16

Chinese

婊子

SKILL PRACTICE

___

Virginia Johnson

Hungarian

Kurva

SKILL PRACTICE

Korean

암캐

SKILL PRACTICE

_____

_____

_____

_____

_____

_____

_____

_____

Virginia Johnson

Japanese

雌犬

SKILL PRACTICE

Finnish

Narttu

SKILL PRACTICE

Czech

Fena

SKILL PRACTICE

Hindi

कुतिया

SKILL PRACTICE

Polish

Suka

SKILL PRACTICE

Somali

Qashin

SKILL PRACTICE

Virginia Johnson

Maltese

Kelba

SKILL PRACTICE

German

Hündin

SKILL PRACTICE

_____

_____

_____

_____

_____

_____

_____

_____

_____

_____

Bosnian

Kučka

(Cock? Nah, Bitch!)

SKILL PRACTICE

_____

_____

_____

_____

_____

_____

_____

_____

_____

_____

English

Bitch

(In case no-one was paying attention)

SKILL PRACTICE

_____

_____

_____

_____

_____

_____

_____

_____

_____

_____

_____

_____

Zulu

i-bitch

(seem pretty modern. Otherwise, the iphone, ipad and ipod have ancestors within the foreign language studies. I-bitch. Maybe this is just self-proclaimed.)

SKILL PRACTICE

Greek

Σκύλα

SKILL PRACTICE

Thai

ผู้หญิงเลว

(This one is pretty!)

SKILL PRACTICE

Estonian

Emane

SKILL PRACTICE

Virginia Johnson

Turkish

Orospu

SKILL PRACTICE

_____

_____

_____

_____

_____

_____

_____

_____

_____

_____

Italian

Cagna

SKILL PRACTICE

Bengali

দুশ্চরিত্রা

(This looks like a lot of work for name calling. Just sayin)

SKILL PRACTICE

Portuguese

Cadela

SKILL PRACTICE

_____

_____

_____

_____

_____

_____

_____

_____

_____

_____

Hmong

Bitch

(simple enough)

SKILL PRACTICE

_____

_____

_____

_____

_____

_____

_____

_____

_____

Kazakh

Ботқа

SKILL PRACTICE

_____

_____

_____

_____

_____

_____

_____

_____

_____

Uzbek

Xashak

SKILL PRACTICE

Icelandic

Tíkur

(I imagine this is how 'tickle' would sound under water)

SKILL PRACTICE

_____

_____

_____

_____

_____

_____

_____

_____

_____

_____

Cebuano

Fasipolo

SKILL PRACTICE

Latin

Bitch

(No time wasted here, either)

SKILL PRACTICE

_____

_____

_____

_____

_____

_____

_____

_____

_____

_____

What have we learned?

Let me tell you...

There are **not** only the ways to say 'bitch' as I have provided you, but numerous other ways to use it. It isn't as universal as FUCK or SHIT, but I am quite sure this entire book will mean nothing to any of you.

As I have promised with every book in this series, there is only so much that we can consider informational. This is not one of them. It certainly could be as long as you are diligent in your approach to using this word. That's a lie, you are probably less intelligent after reading this book.

Keep in mind – a word that we use to identify a person that should be avoided at all costs, is the same word that we use to refer to a dog with a vag. A fucking dog. We evolved to the point that we ran out of things to call each other that we decided a female dog was a huge insult. Better yet, it is only an insult if we give it a cool name. Yeah, someone called their dog 'BITCH' just so they could call the mother of the shitty kid that egged your car, a BITCH.

That is a lot of fucking work to be creative and it paid off. Maybe, just maybe, one of the entitled millennials will donate something to society as cool as 'BITCH'. Wishful thinking, I know.

Anyways... my bitching has come to an end.

Seriously?

I said 'end' and you swiped anyways. You may have proved me wrong and haven't burned precious brain cells while reading this masterpiece. Ok, that was egotistical, but who really gives a fuck? Most people didn't swipe, but you... You are the lucky one that gets to be personally called a bitch. You are the bitch that I knew would keep reading just in case there was more bitching to be done. Touche! A promotion is in order – Status of BIATCH applies to you smart ones that read to the end ;)

Ok... Now I am done.

Coming soon...

ASSH*L*

C*CK

D*CK CH*S*R

And more... I get bored.

About the Author

Virginia is a mom to two beautiful children and resides in Minnesota. Any spare time is spent watching TV, reading, facebooking and spending time with friends.

A love for reading and writing is a new concept for Virginia. Before the Twilight rave and a need to know the ending after Eclipse was released in theaters, Virginia preferred to watch the movie or convince a friend to read the book for her. Needing to know the story of a random homeless man that she encountered on a freeway exit ramp, was the only reason she began writing in the first place. Soulless Nights spawned from the unknown story and a dare from her friends.

She has had the pleasure of working with some of her favorite authors. Street teams, beta reading and cover modeling were what led her to the world of writing.

She currently PA's for Kyle Perkins.

SKILL PRACTICE

SKILL PRACTICE

SKILL PRACTICE

SKILL PRACTICE

SKILL PRACTICE

SKILL PRACTICE

SKILL PRACTICE

SKILL PRACTICE

SKILL PRACTICE

SKILL PRACTICE

SKILL PRACTICE

SKILL PRACTICE

SKILL PRACTICE

SKILL PRACTICE

SKILL PRACTICE

SKILL PRACTICE

SKILL PRACTICE

SKILL PRACTICE

SKILL PRACTICE

SKILL PRACTICE

SKILL PRACTICE

SKILL PRACTICE

SKILL PRACTICE

SKILL PRACTICE

SKILL PRACTICE

SKILL PRACTICE

SKILL PRACTICE

B*TCH

SKILL PRACTICE

SKILL PRACTICE

SKILL PRACTICE

SKILL PRACTICE

SKILL PRACTICE

SKILL PRACTICE

B*TCH

SKILL PRACTICE

SKILL PRACTICE

SKILL PRACTICE

SKILL PRACTICE

SKILL PRACTICE

SKILL PRACTICE

SKILL PRACTICE

SKILL PRACTICE

SKILL PRACTICE

SKILL PRACTICE

SKILL PRACTICE

SKILL PRACTICE

SKILL PRACTICE

SKILL PRACTICE

SKILL PRACTICE

SKILL PRACTICE

SKILL PRACTICE

SKILL PRACTICE

SKILL PRACTICE

SKILL PRACTICE

SKILL PRACTICE

SKILL PRACTICE

SKILL PRACTICE

SKILL PRACTICE

SKILL PRACTICE

SKILL PRACTICE

SKILL PRACTICE

SKILL PRACTICE

SKILL PRACTICE

SKILL PRACTICE

SKILL PRACTICE

SKILL PRACTICE

SKILL PRACTICE

SKILL PRACTICE

SKILL PRACTICE

SKILL PRACTICE

SKILL PRACTICE

SKILL PRACTICE

SKILL PRACTICE

SKILL PRACTICE

Made in the USA
Lexington, KY
18 May 2018